THE CAT
Artlist Collection

BE A COOL CAT!
Purr-fect Advice for Healthy Kids

By The Cats
As told to Apple Jordan

SCHOLASTIC INC.

New York   Toronto   London   Auckland   Sydney
Mexico City   New Delhi   Hong Kong   Buenos Aires

ISBN-13: 978-0-545-01187-7
ISBN-10: 0-545-01187-6

© 2007 artlist INTERNATIONAL

Published by Scholastic Inc. All rights reserved.
SCHOLASTIC and associated logos are trademarks and/or registered trademarks of Scholastic Inc.

12 11 10 9 8 7 6 5 4 3 2   8 9 10 11 12/0

Designed by B.A.D. Design Corp. and Angela Jun
Printed in the U.S.A.
First printing, November 2007

Be a Cool Cat

Every cool cat knows that the key to good health is having good habits. And who is more a creature of habit than a cat? So let us help you set up some good habits now. From eating healthy to exercising, to living stress-free, you could learn a lot from our feline ways.

We cats know that taking good care of yourself means feeling great about yourself, both inside and out. So here's the *cat's meow* on taking care of YOU!

Catnaps

The number one key to good health is getting a good night's sleep. We cats should know. Sleeping tops our list of favorite activities! And we're really good at it, too. We spend most of our day catnapping. Getting enough sleep can mean the difference between feeling ready to pounce or ready to plop. You'd rather feel like a cheetah than a sloth, wouldn't you?

When you sleep, your body is getting the rest it needs. Sleep helps you recharge for the next day. And you're doing more than just sleeping when you get your shut-eye. You're growing and building up your immune system, which can keep you from getting sick. Not to mention the great dreams you have! So we cats don't recommend skimping on sleep. In fact, we can't imagine why you would!

How to Catch Your Zzz's

We cats like to sleep . . . a lot. Did we mention that?
We can spend up to 16 hours a day in dreamland.
People don't need *that* much sleep, but you do need
eight to ten hours of sleep each night to keep focused
and energized the next day. Here are some tips to help
you get the rest you need:

1. Go to sleep at the same time each night, and wake
   up at the same time each morning.
2. Avoid watching television right before bedtime.
   Instead, read a book to help you relax.
3. Avoid foods and drinks that contain caffeine close
   to bedtime.
4. Establish a bedtime routine. Take a bubble bath,
   read, draw, listen to some relaxing music — anything
   that will soothe you
   and help you drift off.

Night Owls—er—Cats

Cats are nocturnal. We like to sleep most of the day and save our energy to play all night. But that doesn't work for kids. Don't make a habit of staying up late. You'll regret it the next day!

Don't Be a Couch Potato

Cats love to exercise. We jump, pounce, prance, leap, and run. It's important for you to stay active, too. When you move around, your blood starts flowing and your heart starts pumping. Exercise gives you energy and keeps your body healthy and strong.

Cats love to watch the great outdoors through the window, so we know that it's important for kids to get out of the house. Too much time inside watching television or playing video games isn't good for the mind or body.

So get outside and start running, biking, hiking, jump roping, or playing tag with friends. You'll have fun and feel great!

Safety First!

Cats have a natural ability to always land on our feet. But that doesn't apply to people! So when you're outside having fun, be safe. When you ride your bike or Rollerblade, be sure to always wear your helmet.

Be a Team Player

Sports are a great way to get exercise *and* have fun. Playing a sport helps you stay fit, builds your confidence and self-esteem, and teaches you discipline. It is also a great way to make new friends.

There are many team sports to choose from—football, baseball, basketball, soccer, and hockey, just to name a few. There are also a lot of solo sports that might be more up your alley, like tae kwon do, running, or swimming. A lot of these solo activities can also be done as part of a team. But whatever sport you choose, make sure it's something that *you* love to do.

And remember: Whatever sport you choose, you don't have to be the best player on the team to have fun and get great exercise!

Cat-letes

If we cats were to participate in a group sport, it would definitely be gymnastics. Our tails help us balance so we can walk on the narrowest beams without fear of falling. One sport we'd steer clear of? Swimming. We hate getting wet!

Dancing Paws

Cats love to dance! We love to hear the music, wave our tails, and tap our paws.

Not.

All right, dancing isn't our thing. But we do know it's a great way for you to get exercise *and* have fun. You can move your body, stomp your feet, and wave your arms. This really gets your heart pumping and blood flowing.

Don't Forget the Warm-up!

We cats love to sink our claws in and s-t-r-e-t-c-h! This helps us stay fit. Stretching should be an important part of your exercise routine, too. Stretching your muscles helps prevent injuries. It's a good idea to warm up and stretch for at least five minutes prior to exercising.

Dancing is also a great way to get creative and express yourself. And there are many different styles of dance to choose from, too.

Salsa  Swing 🐾 Tango 🐾 Modern 🐾 Hip-Hop 🐾 Ballet
Jazz 🐾 African 🐾 Step dancing 🐾 Tap 🐾 Ballroom
Break-dancing 🐾 Square dancing

So next time you want to move your body and feel great, get out there and *cha-cha-cha!*

Cat Food 101

We cats love to eat *almost* as much as we love to sleep. When we hear a can of cat food open, we come running! We know how important our meals are. We would never skip a meal, and neither should you.

Eating gives us energy to do things. And eating the right foods gives us the protein and nutrients we need for a strong and healthy body. What's even better . . . it tastes good, too!

Breakfast Bites

We know you've heard it before: Breakfast is the most important meal of the day. It's true! A balanced breakfast fuels you up for the day ahead. Now you know why we climb on your head in the morning. It's so you'll get up and feed us our breakfast!

The Food Pyramid

Pyramids are something we cats know a lot about. After all, some of our earliest ancestors came from Egypt, the land of the pyramids. All right, those are different pyramids, but we cats can still help you figure out the mysteries of the food pyramid.

There are lots of foods to choose from, but they aren't all equally good for you. Your body needs a variety of foods to stay healthy. Follow these food pyramid guidelines to know how much of each type of food you should eat.

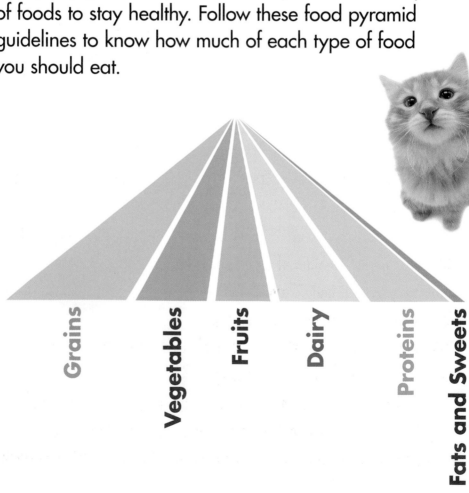

Grains Vegetables Fruits Dairy Proteins Fats and Sweets

Food Group	Daily Servings
Grains	4 to 5 for 4- to 8-year-olds; 5 to 6 for 9- to 13-year-olds
Vegetables	$1\frac{1}{2}$ for 4- to 8-year-olds; $2\text{-}\frac{1}{2}$ for 9- to 13-year-olds
Fruits	1 to $1\text{-}\frac{1}{2}$ for 4- to 8-year-olds; $1\text{-}\frac{1}{2}$ for 9- to 13-year-olds
Dairy	1 to 2 for 4- to 8-year-olds; 3 for 9- to 13-year-olds
Proteins	3 to 4 for 4- to 8-year-olds; 5 for 9- to 13-year-olds
Fats and Sweets	only once in a while

- GRAINS include foods such as bread, cereal, rice, and pasta. Whole grains are the healthiest type of grain!
- There are a variety of VEGETABLES to choose from. Try to eat veggies of all different colors. A rainbow of veggies gives you the most nutrients!
- FRUITS are a sweet and delicious treat. Next time you want a snack, reach for a piece of fruit instead of a candy bar.
- Milk, yogurt, and cheese all belong to the DAIRY group. These foods contain calcium, which helps bones grow strong.
- PROTEIN-rich foods include meat, poultry, eggs, fish, beans, and nuts.
- FATS AND SWEETS should only be eaten once in a while. While cookies, candy, and soda might taste yummy, they don't offer any nutritional value.

Healthy Vittles

We cats love to snack. We visit our food bowls often. But we know to stay away from snacks that are too sweet or filled with empty calories, such as candy or potato chips. They give you only a short supply of energy. When you're hungry for a snack, it's better to reach for something healthy. It will keep you energized longer and offer you more nutrients.

Here are some healthy snack alternatives:

Fruit 🍎 Yogurt 🍎 Granola 🍎 Veggies and dip
Pita with hummus 🍎 Nuts 🍎 Dried apricots 🍎 Raisins
Cheese and crackers 🍎 Toast with peanut butter
Cereal 🍎 Guacamole 🍎 Fruit shakes 🍎 Popcorn

Drink Up!

In addition to a healthy diet, your body needs plenty of water each day. It's a good idea to drink six to eight glasses of water daily. And while you're at it, don't forget to fill up our kitty bowls with clean water, too. That would make us *purr*-fectly happy!

Feline Friendships

We cats sometimes get a bad rap. Sure, some of us can be antisocial. But some of us love cozying up with a pal and being affectionate. And we know that people need a lot of social contact to be happy, too. Friendship is an important part of everyone's life! Good friends make you feel good about yourself. And the key to having good friends is *being* a good friend.

A good friend is someone who . . .

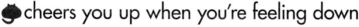
is a good listener

makes time for you

is honest

is considerate of your feelings

makes you laugh

cheers you up when you're feeling down

Feline Friendly

When cats are feeling friendly, they might rub up against your leg. They may also rub noses with another cat to let them know they want to be friends.

Neat Beasts

We cats are fussy felines. We are very neat and spend hours each day cleaning ourselves to make sure our fur looks fabulous. And so should you! Being clean means being healthy. If you feel good about how you look on the outside, chances are you probably feel pretty good on the inside, too.

 Germ Patrol

Not all germs are bad for you, but some germs can be a real nuisance. Here are a few tips to avoid spreading germs, especially during the cold and flu season:

1. Wash your hands regularly.
2. Always cover your mouth when you cough, or your nose when you sneeze.
3. Use a tissue once, then throw it away.

We cats don't have much in our lives to worry about, unless our food bowl is empty! But we know life in the human world can be a bit more stressful. Peer pressure, school, and family might cause you to wish you could catnap the day away. But being worried and anxious can make you sad or even sick!

It's Only Natural

Remember, it's okay to feel the way you do. Everyone feels down once in a while!

When things are tough, you need some ways to help you get through the day. We cats can help! Here are some ideas for helping you deal with stress:

1. Exercise. It isn't just great for the body—it helps release stress, too.
2. Keep a journal. Jotting down what worries you may help you feel better. Before you go to bed at night, write down everything on your mind: a big test the next day, thank-you cards you need to write, basketball tryouts, a fight you had with your best friend. Putting your thoughts on paper will help you sleep better!
3. Get creative. Draw pictures, write poetry, paint, join an acting group. These are all great outlets for relieving stress.
4. Find a quiet spot just for you—your bedroom, a sunny spot outside, a reading corner in the library. Go there to relax and just think about YOU.
5. Talk to someone you trust—your best friend, a parent, a teacher.

We've been told that pets can help reduce stress, too. So hang out with us for a while, and we'll help you relax!

It's All in the Attitude

We cats have a lot of attitude. We can be moody, finicky, or downright unfriendly. But we know that the key to staying healthy is all about having the *right* attitude. Our advice to you? Always try to stay positive!

🐾 Look on the sunny side of things.
🐾 Don't sweat the small stuff.
🐾 Start each day with a smile and a purr.

Dental Hygiene

Your smile is the first thing many people notice about you . . . and you want it to sparkle! To get that *purr*-fect smile, you have to take good care of your pearly whites.

Remember to always . . .
- brush your teeth at least two times a day.
- visit your dentist twice a year.
- replace your toothbrush every three months.
- limit the sweets you eat. They can cause cavities!
- floss every day.

# Clean Up Your Clutter

We cats are neat, and we have our reasons. We like our world to be orderly, or else things can start feeling a little unruly. We know it's the same for kids, too. If you stay organized, you'll feel more in control and better about yourself.

Here are some tips for keeping your life clutter free:

1. Tidy up your room a little each day. That way, things won't pile up, and cleaning won't seem like an overwhelming chore at the end of the week.

2. Find a place for everything. Use storage bins and old boxes to hold clothes, toys, school papers, and all of your odds and ends.

3. Make lists of things you need to do each day and check them off as you go. If you don't get to an item on your list, put it at the top of the next day's list.

4. Lay out your school clothes the night before. This will save you time in the morning so you don't have to rush.

5. Don't procrastinate. If you leave important things to the last minute, you'll stress out and probably not do the best job you can!

Lend a Helping Paw

Taking good care of ourselves can also mean taking care of others. Volunteering is a great way to help others and give back to your community—and the big bonus is that you just might feel pretty good about yourself, too! While making a difference in your community, you'll have the opportunity to meet people, learn new skills, and have fun.

Here are some suggestions for how you can volunteer in your community:

- Walk a neighbor's dog.
- Help a younger child learn to read.
- Volunteer at a local retirement home.
- Donate your old clothes and toys to charity.
- Help clean up your local park.
- Help grow a community garden.

There is no one more important than you, so be sure to take good care of yourself, both inside and out. We hope we've given you plenty of ideas on how to treat yourself well and leave you *feline* fine!

The Cats